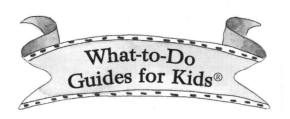

What-to-Do
Guides for Kids®

What to Do
When You Feel

Too sHy

A Kid's Guide to
Overcoming Social Anxiety

by Claire A. B. Freeland, PhD,
and Jacqueline B. Toner, PhD

illustrated by Janet McDonnell

MAGINATION PRESS • WASHINGTON, DC
AMERICAN PSYCHOLOGICAL ASSOCIATION

Published by
MAGINATION PRESS®
An Educational Publishing Foundation Book
American Psychological Association
750 First Street, NE
Washington, DC 20002

Magination Press is a registered trademark of the American Psychological Association.

For more information about our books, including a complete catalog, please write to us, call 1-800-374-2721, or visit our website at www.apa.org/pubs/magination.

Book design by Sandra Kimbell
Printed by Worzalla, Stevens Point, WI

Library of Congress Cataloging-in-Publication Data

Names: Freeland, Claire A. B., author. | Toner, Jacqueline B., author. | McDonnell, Janet, 1962– illustrator.
Title: What to do when you feel too shy : a kid's guide to overcoming social anxiety / by Claire A. B. Freeland, PhD, and Jacqueline B. Toner, PhD ; illustrated by Janet McDonnell.
Description: Washington, DC : Magination Press, 2016. | Series: What-to-do guides for kids | Audience: Age 6-12.
Identifiers: LCCN 2016005470| ISBN 9781433822766 (pbk.) | ISBN 1433822768 (pbk.)
Subjects: LCSH: Anxiety in children—Juvenile literature. | Anxiety—Juvenile literature.
Classification: LCC BF723.A5 .f74 2016 | DDC 155.4/18232—dc23
LC record available at http://lccn.loc.gov/2016005470

Manufactured in the United States of America
10 9 8 7 6 5 4 3 2 1

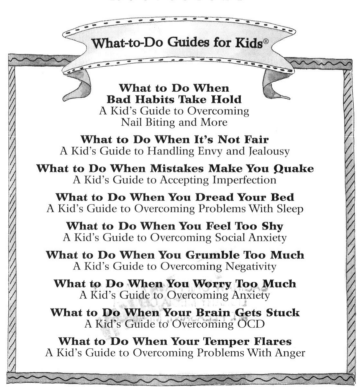

What-to-Do Guides for Kids®

What to Do When Bad Habits Take Hold
A Kid's Guide to Overcoming
Nail Biting and More

What to Do When It's Not Fair
A Kid's Guide to Handling Envy and Jealousy

What to Do When Mistakes Make You Quake
A Kid's Guide to Accepting Imperfection

What to Do When You Dread Your Bed
A Kid's Guide to Overcoming Problems With Sleep

What to Do When You Feel Too Shy
A Kid's Guide to Overcoming Social Anxiety

What to Do When You Grumble Too Much
A Kid's Guide to Overcoming Negativity

What to Do When You Worry Too Much
A Kid's Guide to Overcoming Anxiety

What to Do When Your Brain Gets Stuck
A Kid's Guide to Overcoming OCD

What to Do When Your Temper Flares
A Kid's Guide to Overcoming Problems With Anger

CONTENTS

Introduction to Parents and Caregivers

One of the joys of parenting is seeing your child become a separate and unique individual, with his or her own personality and style. No longer dependent on you for every little thing, your child takes on the world standing on his or her own two feet. But what about children who are socially anxious? What about children who don't have the social confidence to assert themselves or who have trouble joining in with others? It can be hard to see your child refuse to attend a birthday party, for example, or not participate in activities that other children seem to embrace without hesitation.

While every child—every human—experiences shy feelings on occasion, some children are more frequently self-conscious and reticent than others. They overestimate the threat of being embarrassed or rejected. And they experience real distress as a result. Their brains and bodies send off sirens of alarm when they are in certain social situations.

While it can be easy to classify such children as shy, it is important to note that shyness and social anxiety are not the same thing. While many shy children experience social anxiety, many do not, and not all children with social anxiety are shy. Children who enter unfamiliar social situations with some wariness or who are self-conscious when they perceive they are being evaluated by others are considered shy. This mild to moderate degree of shyness is characteristic of many children. These children may take longer to adjust in specific situations, but they warm up and join in. Children with social anxiety, on the other hand, are significantly fearful and embarrassed in social evaluative situations, so much so that they experience high distress or avoid these settings altogether.

So where does social anxiety come from? There are no definitive answers. In most cases, there is probably a combination of factors, including a biological vulnerability to becoming anxious. Other factors, such as the behavior of role models, cultural differences, and a variety of early experiences, can contribute. Yet, no matter the cause, children can acquire the practice and skills that help them grow in social confidence.

It's stressful to have trouble with everyday activities, such as joining in a conversation, answering a question in class, ordering in a restaurant, attending typical extracurricular activities, and performing, even as part of a group. And, if your child struggles with social anxiety, you are all too aware of what happens when your child feels in the spotlight: chills, dizziness, trembling, flushing, and so forth. You have probably wrestled with your child's repeated refusals to participate and experienced their pleading, their tantrums, and their acceptance of punishment just as long as they don't have to engage in the dreaded activity.

Not only do your child and family suffer in those moments, but your child loses out on important experiences that contribute to development. Social confidence not only feels better; it's useful. Socially confident kids are more successful in school. They get along well with peers, take on more challenges, and receive more support from others.

If your son or daughter is far from socially confident, take heart. *What to Do*

When You Feel Too Shy will guide your child on a path to greater comfort in social settings. The approach, which is based on cognitive-behavioral principles, combines several elements:

- practicing social skills, such as greetings, asking questions, and responding to others;
- assertiveness training, including speaking up for oneself;
- gradual exposure to tough situations, taking on more independence in various settings;
- new ways of thinking, learning what confident children say to themselves;
- problem-solving skills when things don't go as hoped; and
- emotional self-regulation to handle stress.

Through a variety of activities and opportunities for practice, your child will learn to speak up, join in and participate, and expand his or her comfort zone through experiencing step-by-step success.

Although this book is written for your child, its success depends on your involvement. When your child is young, you have a great opportunity to coach the kinds of behaviors that will help him or her overcome social anxiety. We suggest you begin by reading through the entire book on your own. Then read the book together with your child, taking it slowly, a chapter at a time. Encourage your child to do the exercises along the way, and talk together about how the examples and practice from the book apply in real life. There is a lot for your child to absorb and plenty to practice. Give your child ample praise for any and every effort. Change is built on a platform of tiny steps.

If you have found that social anxiety has gotten in your way before, you may recognize many of the book's examples in your own past experience. Talk with your child about your coping strategies and how you managed to keep your anxiety from interfering in your life. If you rarely experience anxiety in social situations, work hard to understand your child's perspective. Your empathy and patience will go a long way toward helping your child feel supported and more willing to take risks.

No matter what your personal experience has been, here are some useful suggestions for you to help your child find healthy ways to cope with social anxiety:

- Prepare your child for new experiences and ease the way through difficult transitions.
- Acknowledge your child's feelings and demonstrate your acceptance.
- Expose your child to a variety of new experiences at a comfortable pace.
- Support and nurture your child's talents and interests.
- Be a role model for friendliness and social graces.
- Stay calm and communicate confidence in your child.

Most socially reserved children become less inhibited in time; however, some children who are hampered by social anxiety are at risk for related difficulties, such as additional worries or fears, irritability, or sleep problems. You may find other books in the **What-to-Do Guides for Kids** series useful to address these concerns. Consult with your pediatrician or mental health professional for evaluation or additional resources if difficulties persist.

Ready to take some time out from the usual three-ring circus of family life for some parent-child time to start building social confidence? Enjoy this time with your child because pretty soon he or she will be off with friends and busy with new activities.

CHAPTER ONE

Clowning Around

When you go to the circus, you almost always see clowns. They perform tricks and make us laugh. They wear bright colors, big shoes, and all kinds of wigs and colorful hats.

One thing is for sure: clowns bring a lot of attention on themselves with their lively costumes and silly antics. Have you noticed that they seem to like people looking at them and laughing at them?

There may be times when you enjoy having others focus on you, but also times when you don't. At those times, you may not feel comfortable having the spotlight focused on you. Lots of kids feel shy when they believe that other people notice them, and those feelings are okay. Feelings are an important part of who you are. Even the ones that feel uncomfortable.

But some kids get super uncomfortable being in the spotlight. It seems their minds and bodies feel too shy or nervous too often. The problem is being too shy in front of other people can really get in your way at times.

Besides making you feel uncomfortable, when you have strong feelings of embarrassment or worries about others laughing at you or criticizing you, you might not join in on cool activities and you might miss the fun. You could end up feeling left out or lonely.

These kinds of feelings might keep you from getting what you want or need.

Do you remember times when being in the spotlight made you feel way too shy? Have any of these situations happened to you?

- You knew an answer in class, but you didn't raise your hand.

- Or maybe you felt too shy to join the ice skating team even though you're a good skater.

- Or the party sounded like fun, but you decided not to go because you were nervous that there might be kids there you didn't know.

- Maybe you didn't buy the item you wanted because you felt too uncomfortable to ask the sales person to help you find it.

9

Maybe there were other times when your worries about other people's attention were a problem for you.

Write or draw about a time that you felt too shy.

To keep your worries about being in the spotlight from getting too strong, you need to learn different ways of handling yourself. It won't happen all at once. By taking small steps, you'll make progress and begin to work around feeling too shy. You'll get more confident being around other people. And you'll find the spotlight isn't so bad after all.

CHAPTER TWO

Lion Taming

Some circuses have lions that do tricks. They sit on platforms, moving from one to another when the lion tamer cracks his whip. They may even jump through hoops.

The lion tamer is not afraid because he has learned how to get the lions to perform. But if you were asked to come pet the lion, you would be afraid! That's a good thing because petting lions is not safe unless you have worked for years to learn how to train lions. When we are in unsafe situations, our hearts beat faster, we shake, our muscles tighten. This is how our bodies alert us to danger. And that's helpful because we pay attention to these signals and we get ourselves to safety.

Sometimes our bodies respond this way when there is no lion, and nothing else that can hurt us. This is called ANXieTY. Often, people experience ANXieTY in their bodies just like a fear reaction. ANXieTY can sneak up on you.

Remember the first chapter, when you read about feeling uncomfortable being in the spotlight? Your body may react with ANXieTY when you feel too shy or embarrassed or uncomfortable around people.

Different people can feel ANXiETY in different parts of their bodies. Take a look at this drawing of a person. Circle where you usually feel ANXiETY when people are watching you or you have to talk in front of others—when you are in the spotlight:

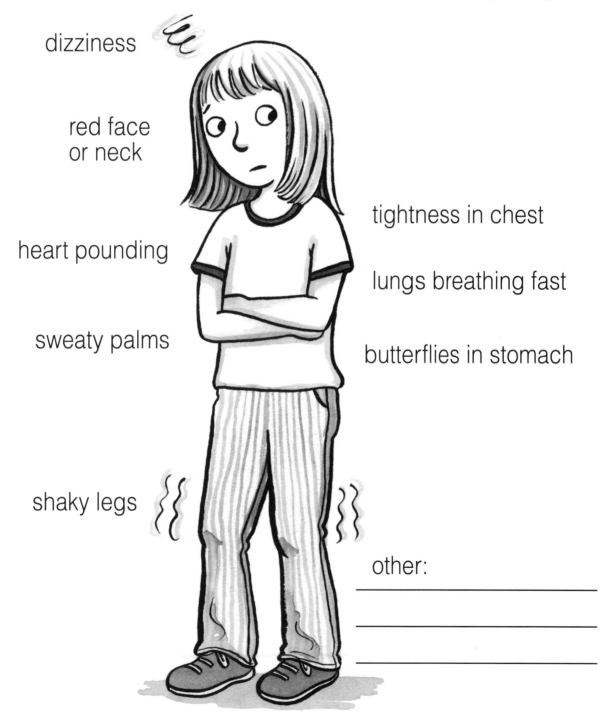

dizziness

red face or neck

heart pounding

sweaty palms

shaky legs

tightness in chest

lungs breathing fast

butterflies in stomach

other:

_____

_____

_____

Most people have anxiety about being the center of attention in some situations.

Look at the list below. Which of the situations below make you feel anxious?

- ☐ Being called on in school to answer a question or read aloud
- ☐ Giving a report to the class
- ☐ Going up to the blackboard or smart board to write
- ☐ Working on a project at school in a small group
- ☐ Going up to a group of kids on the playground and joining in
- ☐ Attending a group activity like an ice cream social or other event
- ☐ Coming into class late
- ☐ Using the bathroom at a friend's house

- ☐ Going to a neighbor's house to pick up something for your mom or dad

- ☐ Answering the phone

- ☐ Ordering food in a restaurant

- ☐ Making a phone call to a friend

- ☐ Attending an activity outside of school

- ☐ Performing in a recital

- ☐ Asking a friend to get together

- ☐ Starting a conversation

- ☐ Talking to adults

- ☐ Paying a cashier

Which situations did you check off?

Notice that none of them are truly dangerous—not like petting a lion! But your body reacts as if there was some danger.

The situations that usually make you feel anxious are called TRiGGers.

These TRiGGer situations lead to WORRy THoUGHTs, which produce the anxious Feelings. Then, you may feel too shy to do something and you may try to get out of the situation.

It's like a chain reaction. Each link in the chain causes the next one to happen.

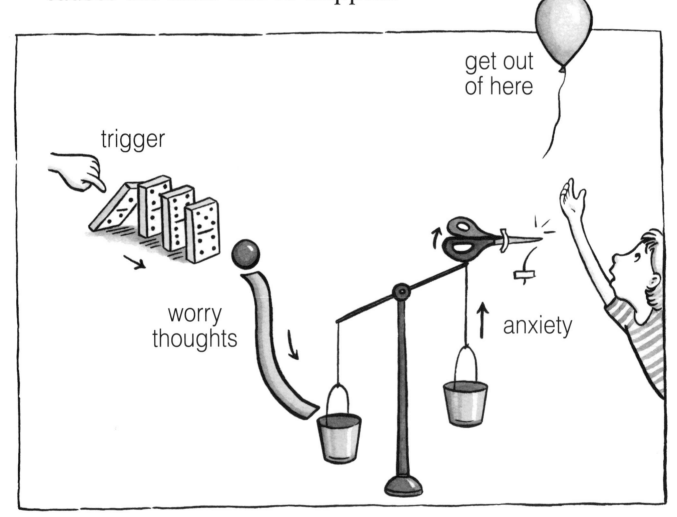

So what are these WORRY THOUGHTS? Here are some common ones:

- "Everyone will laugh at me."
- "They won't like me."
- "I won't know what to say."
- "The kids will see that I'm nervous."

Those WORRY THOUGHTS are certainly going to create aNXieTY! And when someone has those thoughts and the feelings that go with them, what will happen? What will the person probably do?

They might:

- Stay quiet.
- Try to leave.
- Look down.
- Say no to fun activities.

So you see how a TRiGGeR situation leads to WORRY THOUGHTS, which lead to aNXieTY that might cause you to miss out on important accomplishments or fun.

If you avoid situations because you are trying to escape your ᴀɴxɪᴏᴜꜱ ꜰᴇᴇʟɪɴɢꜱ, it might help to know that you are not alone. Everyone feels too shy sometimes and many kids get ᴀɴxɪᴏᴜꜱ when the spotlight is on them. Here's the good news: there are skills and strategies that can help. After learning these skills, many kids feel less ᴀɴxɪᴏᴜꜱ than they used to!

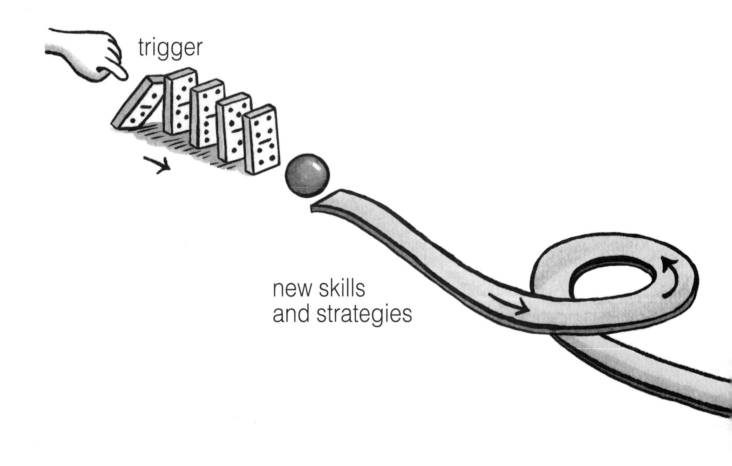

trigger

new skills and strategies

Want to change the chain reaction? When you change what you think and what you do, you can "tame that lion" and change your aNxieTY!

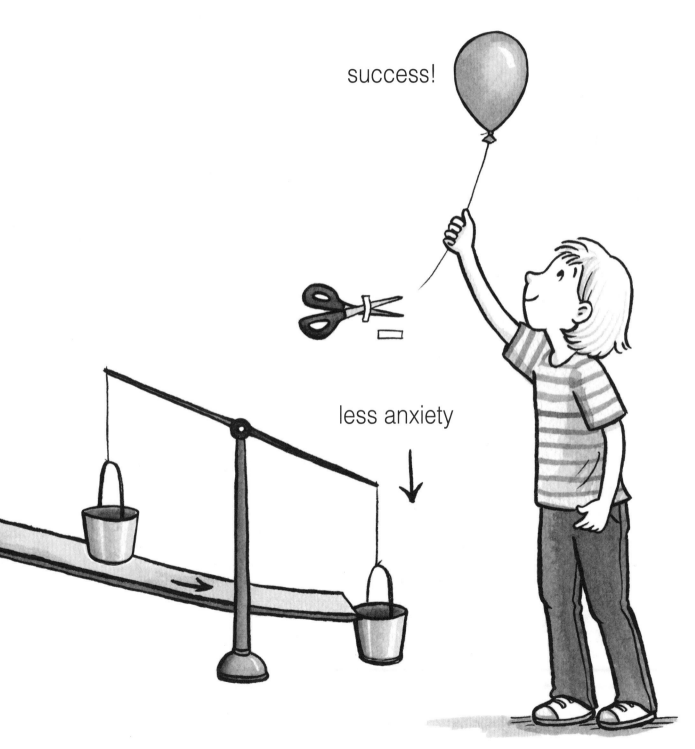

success!

less anxiety

CHAPTER THREE

In the Spotlight

Circus performers need many different skills and strategies to put on a show. Can you imagine if a juggler thought to himself, "I'll never be able to juggle all these pins! I'm going to drop them and everyone in the audience will laugh at me!" Those WORRY THOUGHTS might make him so ANXIOUS that he gives up and avoids performing!

I'll never get this.

But what if the juggler changes his WORRY THOUGHTS? He could think to himself, "I've got this. Everyone will be having so much fun at the circus. Even if I drop a pin, people will still enjoy the show." Do you think those thoughts would encourage him to try? This chapter will teach you some ways to identify your WORRY THOUGHTS and challenge them with CONFIDENT THOUGHTS, so you can step into the spotlight and shine!

Hey, I'm still pretty good!

Here are some of the WORRY THOUGHTS kids have that can lead to ANXIOUS feelings:

- "I won't know what to say."
- "She probably doesn't want to play with me."
- "They won't like my oral report."
- "Everyone will see that I'm shaking."
- "I'll probably mess it up."

These kinds of thoughts are negative and make it more likely that someone will feel ANXIOUS. There are different types of WORRY THOUGHTS. A few common ones are: SPOTLIGHT THOUGHTS, MIND-READING THOUGHTS, and SELF-DOUBTING THOUGHTS.

Lunch in the cafeteria was a hard time of day for Zoey. She was certain that her classmates were watching her eat. She was so worried about talking with food in her mouth that she stayed quiet. Zoey's thoughts made her feel that there was a spotlight on her. When you have SPOTLIGHT THOUGHTS, you think people are noticing you more than they really are.

Tyler missed a goal in lacrosse. For the rest of the game, he was sure his teammates and the

spectators were all thinking he was a terrible player. It was as if he believed he could read other people's minds. When you have MiND-REaDiNG THoUGHTs, you assume you know what other people are thinking.

Andrew was chosen for student council, but he refused the position. He thought he would not be good at the job. He would not have any good ideas. He would not be able to remember what to report back to his class after the meetings. Andrew's

thoughts made him feel he would disappoint everyone. When you have SeLF-DouBTiNG THoUGHTs, you think you're not good enough.

SPOTLIGHT THOUGHTS, MIND-READING THOUGHTS, and SELF-DOUBTING THOUGHTS make ANXIETY stronger. These kinds of thoughts are unreasonable and unhelpful. But you can use CONFIDENT THOUGHTS to challenge your unreasonable thoughts and help you feel less ANXIOUS.

Help Zoey, Tyler, and Andrew challenge their unreasonable thoughts with CONFIDENT THOUGHTS.

For example, Zoey could try thinking, "People are paying attention to what I'm saying, not to my eating." Can you think of other CONFIDENT THOUGHTS Zoey could use to challenge her SPOTLIGHT THOUGHTS?

_____

_____

_____

_____

_____

_____

26

Instead of Tyler's MiND-ReaDiNG THOUGHTs, he could think to himself, "The spectators are probably thinking about the game, not just about me." Can you think of other CONFiDeNT THOUGHTs for Tyler?

_____

_____

_____

_____

_____

When Andrew has SeLF-DOUBTiNG THOUGHTs, he could tell himself, "Everybody messes up sometimes, but I usually do a good job." What other CONFiDeNT THOUGHTs could Andrew use?

_____

_____

_____

_____

_____

Search for CONFIDENT THOUGHTS when you have unreasonable WORRY THOUGHTS.

Try this maze.

Help the juggler find the pins. Don't let SPOTLIGHT THOUGHTS, MIND-READING THOUGHTS, and SELF-DOUBTING THOUGHTS block your way.

CONFIDENT THOUGHTS help reduce ANXIETY and make it easier to step into the spotlight and get on with the show.

And there's more good news: the things that make you ANXIOUS get easier with practice.

spot-light thoughts

mind-reading thoughts

self-doubting thoughts

confident thoughts

29

CHAPTER FOUR

Up, Up, and Away

Most circus performers need a lot of courage. The tightrope walkers risk falling from tiny wires suspended near the ceiling. Trapeze artists swing back and forth above the ground while hanging by their feet. Of course, none of these performers started out by doing their hardest tricks. They started with simple tricks and, once they had gained skills and overcome their fears, they challenged themselves to do more and more.

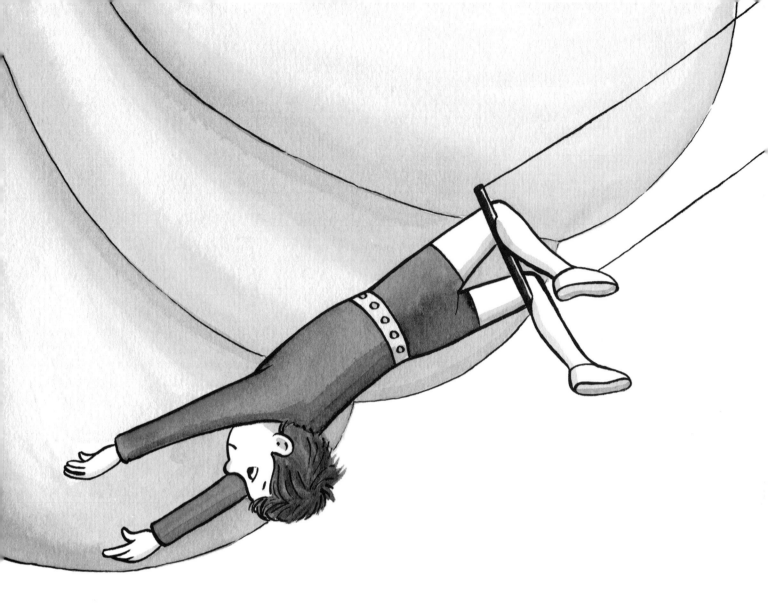

Overcoming ᴀɴxɪᴏᴜꜱ feelings works in the same way. You can get more comfortable in situations that make you feel ᴀɴxɪᴏᴜꜱ by practicing the very things that make you feel that way. But just like a trapeze artist in the circus, you don't need to start with the thing that's most difficult.

Whenever Kendra was asked to spend the night at a friend's house, she would say "no." Her mother noticed that Kendra seemed sad when the other girls would have a sleepover. She kept telling Kendra she should go. But Kendra was just too anxious. She was afraid that a friend's family would have weird food for dinner and that she would be embarrassed to tell them she didn't like it. She worried the other girls would say her pajamas were dorky or talk about things she didn't know anything about and she would feel uncomfortable. She was nervous that she would feel scared in a strange house and would have to talk to an adult about it. She thought she might get so afraid that she would cry and everyone would stare at her.

Much of what Kendra was afraid of had to do with telling other people what she felt or needed. Kendra was feeling a lot of ᴀɴxiᴇᴛy. Of course, not all of the things she was afraid of were equally scary.

With her mom's help, Kendra decided to start by practicing part of a sleepover, a part that made her just a little uncomfortable. She made plans to eat dinner at her friend Cassie's house. Her mom talked to Cassie's mom and asked her not to fix anything special for dinner. Kendra and her mom talked about how to politely tell people if she didn't like something they were serving.

On the day she was supposed to go to Cassie's house, Kendra was pretty nervous. She was even more nervous when her mom dropped her off, and she had trouble relaxing while she and Cassie played. At dinner, Kendra realized that that Cassie's family was having peas with the meal. Lots of kids like peas, but Kendra doesn't. She could feel her stomach getting tight and her hands sweating but she used a loud enough voice to say, "No, thank you, I don't care for peas."

When her mom picked her up, Kendra told her about her great success. She knew that she would still be nervous the next time she went to a friend's house for dinner, but she also knew she would be less afraid and would know what to do if she were served something she didn't like. Her mom told Kendra that she was very proud of her.

Why will Kendra be less afraid next time she eats at a friend's house? And how will this help her become brave enough eventually to go to a sleepover party? Why does it help to practice what you're afraid to do?

Remember all the ways in which your body can respond when you feel aNxioUs (like your palms sweat and your face turns red)? Well, if you stay long enough in a situation that makes you feel aNxioUs, your body gets used to it and it calms down. Then, the next time you are in a similar situation, your body won't get quite as upset. If you keep practicing, eventually your body may stop sending those fear signals altogether.

Make a list of times when you feel too shy, or situations you might say "no" to because of aNxieTY. Some might involve having to talk to different kinds of people, like adults you know, strangers, or other kids. Some might include doing things in front of other people that you don't think you do well or have never done before. Some might involve saying you don't like something or asking for help. Make the list as long as you can. Here's a list that Carter wrote:

Carter's List

- Invite a friend to go somewhere
- Go to a sleepover party
- Say hello to the checkout person at the supermarket
- Buy something without adult help
- Order food from a drive-up window
- Ask an adult where the bathroom is at the library
- Tell the teacher that you don't understand how to do your homework
- Order pizza over the phone
- Ask some kids on the playground if they'd like to play with you

Your List

- _____
- _____
- _____
- _____
- _____
- _____
- _____
- _____
- _____
- _____
- _____
- _____

Now, put your list on a ladder with the hardest thing at the top and the least hard at the bottom.

The next challenge is to start working your way up that ladder. Most kids take one step at a time and the first step, although it seems like the easiest thing to do, is often the hardest. You will find that, as you climb higher up the ladder, the steps further up start to look easier than they did at first. If that happens, it's okay to skip steps or do more than one at once. You can also repeat any step if you need to until your aNxieTY is less intense.

Remember that when you try something that makes you feel aNxioUs, uncomfortable reactions in your body will start to go away as you get used to the situation. So go ahead and take that first step. Soon you'll be climbing that ladder and flying high!

House of Mirrors

Have you ever visited a house of mirrors at the circus? There are many different kinds of mirrors and you see yourself differently in each one. There might be one that makes you look super tall, another that makes you short and wide, and still others that make you look like you are upside down or make your face look like a cartoon character with a gigantic mouth. It's funny to see yourself in all these different ways. But even though you look different in each kind of mirror, you know that you are the same person in each one!

Being around other people can be like a house of mirrors—it can seem as if you're a different you with different people. But even though you might act differently with different people, you are the same you each time. Sometimes, you might feel anxious and avoid doing things because you feel too shy, but not at other times. And, yet, you are always you!

Kids who feel too shy a lot are sometimes unsure about how to act around other people. You probably feel relaxed and comfortable around some people and less so around others.

What do you do when you are around someone you are comfortable with? You might smile, talk, look at the other person, or show interest in what he or she is saying. These behaviors are all part of being friendly.

When you feel aNxioUs around others, you might not look as friendly as you do when you are comfortable—but that is just a trick mirror! You are still the same person inside. There are ways to look and sound friendly even if you feel uneasy. Practice being friendly so you can use these skills when you start to feel aNxioUs. **Step one** in being friendly is greeting someone. Here are some ways to do it:

- Stand up straight.

- Look at the person.

- Smile.

- Say hello.

Step two is starting a conversation. Here are some ways to start a conversation with another kid:

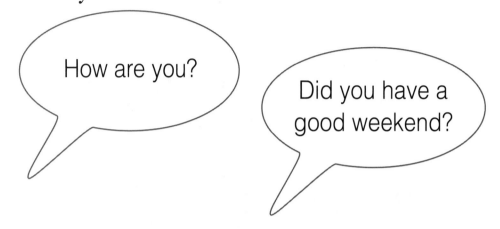

How are you?

Did you have a good weekend?

Now it's your turn. What else could you ask?

_____

_____

_____

_____

_____

_____

Once you are talking to someone, it will help to have some skills for keeping a conversation going. Here are the basic skills that you need:

- **Take turns.** Some people do too much of the talking. In a conversation, you need to be a talker and a listener.

- **Respond to the topic.** Some people start talking about what's on their minds instead of responding to what the other person is saying. You don't have to talk about the same topic for the whole time, but make sure to listen to the person talking and respond to what he or she is saying.

- **Ask questions.** When you ask the other person a question, you are showing an interest in them.

- **Make comments.** Commenting on what the other person is saying is another way to show interest.

Noah doesn't usually feel ᗩИᕼIOᑌᔕ about talking to other kids, but Lily does. One Monday morning, he comes to school and spots Lily. He says, "I saw *The Boys From Mars* movie this weekend. Have you seen it?"

Lily feels ᗩИᕼIOᑌᔕ. She looks down and replies, "No."

Noah tries again, "It was great. You should see it." Lily doesn't know what to say, so she doesn't say anything. Noah turns his attention to someone else.

Let's help Lily have a conversation with Noah.

How can Lily respond when Noah says, "I saw *The Boys From Mars* movie this weekend. Have you seen it?"

Write a friendly response.

Charlotte's grandparents have just arrived for a visit. They live in another city and don't get to see her often. Charlotte feels ᴀɴxious about talking to them.

Help Charlotte give her grandparents a polite and friendly greeting. What should she do?

1. _____

2. _____

3. _____

4. _____

What are some things she could ask or say to start a conversation?

1. _____

2. _____

3. _____

4. _____

Charlotte might continue to feel **anxious** for a while, but when she acts friendly, her grandparents will probably act friendly also, which will help her feel more comfortable. Did you know that scientists have found that when people smile, they actually feel happier? You smile when you're happy, but you also get happy when you smile.

Practice your greeting and conversation skills and pretty soon your friendliness will be reflected back in the great reactions you get from others!

CHAPTER SIX

The Ringmaster

The circus ringmaster introduces the circus and runs the show. The person who gets that job has to be great at SPEAKING UP no matter who is listening. Each person needs to be their own ringmaster and SPEAK UP for themselves. What does SPEAKING UP mean? It means telling someone what you want or need in a polite but definite way. There are times when it's important to speak up to let other people know what you want or what you like or what you don't. You might not always get what you want, but if you don't SPEAK UP, you certainly won't get what you want.

Luis is getting his lunch in the school cafeteria and the lunch lady hands him a banana instead of the apple that he wants. SPEAKING UP is saying, "Excuse me, may I have an apple instead?"

Maya is at a birthday party. Kids are taking turns on the slide. She notices that a few kids have already gotten a second turn and she has not had a first turn yet. SPEAKING UP is saying, "It's my turn next, please."

SPEAKING UP can be hard if ANXIOUS feelings get in the way.

What are some of the reasons it can be hard to speak up?

One reason is worry about other people's reactions. You can practice what to say in different situations and be ready to speak up, but you can't know for sure how other people will respond. Not knowing how others will react can make speaking up hard.

Some kids think that if they speak up, others will make fun of them or be angry. So they say nothing.

Remember that you have a right to speak up. How other people respond to you does not mean you shouldn't speak up. In the next chapter, we'll give you some skills for handling other people's reactions, but for now let's look at some speaking up guidelines.

* Use a loud enough voice.
* Stand tall.
* Be polite.

There are lots of opportunities to speak up at school.

What can you say when someone is stepping in front of you in line?

You might say, "Excuse me but the end of the line is back there."

What can you say when you are not finished using something and someone else is trying to take it from you?

_____

_____

_____

_____

_____

What can you say when you want to sit down at the lunch table and there are belongings on the chair?

_____

_____

_____

_____

_____

There are also plenty of chances to speak up when you are at a friend's house.

What can you say when your friend's dad offers you a snack you don't like?

You might say, "I'm sorry, Mr. Johnson, but I don't really like bananas. May I have something else, please?"

What can you say when your friend won't let you help decide what you are going to play?

_____

_____

_____

_____

_____

What can you say when your friend's parents are allowing a movie you know your parents would not want you to watch?

_____

_____

_____

_____

_____

Life is full of situations in which it will be important for you to **SPEAK UP**. You cannot control other people, but you can be your own ringmaster. You can tell people what you need and what you think and what's okay with you and what's not okay.

Most of the time, others will appreciate your message. But people whose ANXIOUS feelings get in the way may have to practice their SPEAKING UP skills. So, step right up, folks, and start practicing!

Expect the Unexpected

Circus performers spend lots of time working on their acts, choosing their costumes, checking their props, and training their animals, but sometimes it just doesn't go as planned.

Just like a performer in the circus, you will sometimes have to deal with the unexpected as you work to overcome your aNxieTY. If you've spent a lot of time planning what you can say to people, it can be frustrating if they don't respond the way that you hope. It can hurt your feelings if you overcome your aNxieTY to invite someone to join you in an activity and they say "no." But it's important not to get too discouraged when things don't turn out the way you expected.

When making a plan to try something that makes you feel aNXiOUs, you should also take time to think about what might go wrong and what you might do if there's a problem.

? What if you invite a friend to go to the movies and she says "no?"

? What if you tell your teacher you need help with math and he says, "Look at the problem again?"

? What if you go to a bowling party and all the other kids are much better at bowling than you?

? What if you ask to join a group on the playground and they don't let you?

? What if a salesperson gets frustrated with how long it takes you to get the right coins out to pay for a candy bar?

These kinds of worries may sound familiar. But there's a difference between just worrying about something not turning out well and coming up with a plan about what to do. Worrying just leads to ɑnxious Feelings. If you plan ahead to deal with challenging situations, you will have some constructive ways to deal with them and can make good choices about how to react.

Jake finds out that some of the other boys in his class were invited to play paintball for Daniel's birthday. Jake wasn't invited. His feelings are hurt, but he decides to come up with a plan to deal with this problem. He thinks about his choices:

Jake thinks about what might happen for each choice and how he would feel. He thinks about saying nothing at all, but that doesn't feel very good. Instead, Jake decides to ask Daniel and Joe to go rock climbing on another day.

You might feel frustrated, hurt, mad, or embarrassed when other people do things that you don't like. Sometimes those feelings can be strong. When that happens, it's a good idea to stop and think about your choices, just like Jake did. That's called an

Let's practice.

1. A kid in school calls you "Wimpy."
   You could:

   a. Ignore her.

   B. Tell her that she hurt your feelings.

   C. Laugh.

   D. Call her "Stumpy."

   e. _____

2. You have a birthday party and two of your favorite friends say they can't come.
   You could:

   a. Ask them why they aren't coming.

   B. Stop being friendly towards them.

   C. Cancel the party.

   D. Invite two other people.

   e. _____

3. You are trying to overcome your aNxieTY and are waiting to ask your soccer coach a question but he's ignoring you.
You could:

   a. Walk away and try another day.

   B. Say "Excuse me, Mr. Brown" in a loud enough voice.

   C. Jump up and down and say "Mr. Brown, Mr. Brown."

   D. Ask your dad to talk to Mr. Brown for you.

   e. _____

4. You're getting a drink of water from the fountain when you get bumped hard from behind and water goes down your front.
You could:

   a. Say "Be careful! You got me soaked!"

   B. Complain to the teacher that the kids pushed you.

   C. Walk away and say nothing.

   D. Splash water at the kid behind you.

   e. _____

Some of these answers are better than others.

Once you've made a list of your choices, take a minute to think about what might happen after you do each one. That will help you decide which choice works best.

In Jake's case, he really wanted to be better friends with Daniel and the other boys. He decided that getting angry or saying nothing wouldn't help. Instead, he tried to think of a fun activity he could invite his friends to do.

The better you get at taking an iNTeRMiSSioN to think through ways you can respond to unexpected, upsetting, or hurtful experiences, the better able you will be to overcome aNXiouS feelings.

CHAPTER EIGHT

Sit Back, Relax, and Enjoy the Show

While you are at the circus enjoying the acts, the tightrope walkers are concentrating hard on every step. Each member of the circus has a job to do that takes focus and care.

You are like a circus performer when you are challenging WORRY THOUGHTS, trying things that make you feel anxious, and practicing your friendly skills. You have to focus on what you are doing and saying. Performing puts your body in a stress mode. Stress is good when it helps you concentrate and work hard towards your goals. Tightrope walkers' muscles are tight so they aren't wobbly as they move across the tightrope. They are breathing hard and paying attention every step of the way.

But no one can keep that up all the time. After the circus, the performers need ways to relax and rid their bodies of stress. You need that too. We all do.

Relaxing can be active or it can be quietly creative. You can relax alone or with others. It helps to have a variety of ways to let off steam. Think about what you like to do to unwind. Each of the lists below gives you ideas of how some kids relax. Fill in the lists with activities that work for you:

Move

Ride my bike
Go swimming
Jump rope

_____

_____

_____

Make

Draw
Use clay
Build something

_____

_____

_____

Connect

Play with a friend
Play cards with Mom or Dad
Video chat with Aunt Susie

_____

_____

_____

Chill

Read a book
Take a bath
Listen to music

_____

_____

_____

Finding ways to relax and calm yourself will help you recover from the stresses of situations that trigger your aNxieTy.

It can also be helpful to "have a talk with yourself" before you enter a stressful situation. Do you think tightrope walkers say to themselves "I'll probably fall today?" Let's hope not! More likely, they are reminding themselves:

"I know what I'm doing." Or, "I've had plenty of practice."

What do you say to yourself when you are practicing speaking up or being friendly? Try encouraging yourself. Look at yourself in the mirror. Give yourself a pep talk. Here are some examples:

Carey, you have a friendly smile.

Jeremy, it doesn't matter that you are quiet at first because after a little bit, you're super fun to be with.

Travis, the last time you spoke up, it went well. You can do it!

What might you say to yourself? Remember to make encouraging statements that are true about you.

All About You

Doing what you find relaxing and giving yourself pep talks will help you de-stress and will encourage you to meet your goals. Then you really can sit back, relax, and enjoy your life!

CHAPTER NINE

You Can Do It!

Although everyone feels anxious at times, anxiety doesn't have to get in the way of what you need to do or the people you want to spend time with. It takes some practice, but anxiety can be tamed. You can use CONFIDENT THOUGHTS to replace WORRY THOUGHTS and help keep your balance, even if you feel a little shaky at first. By challenging untrue thoughts with encouraging thoughts, you'll help yourself feel better.

Of course, just like a performer in the circus, you'll need to practice the skills you've just learned in order to get better at them. That means practicing being friendly and speaking up for yourself in a polite way. And, of course, you'll need to practice thinking ahead of time about what to do if you get disappointed. It will take time to get really good at these skills so be kind and patient with yourself.

When you need to calm down and relax, you now know you can.

Great job! Write your name on this circus poster to join the circus of fun and friends!